My Dad's Deployment

A deployment and reunion

Activity Book

for young children

An Elva Resa book

Written by Julie LaBelle ★ Illustrated by Christina Rodriguez

★ A note to parents, teachers, and caregivers ★

The activities in this book are meant to help young children express their thoughts and feelings while they have a parent deployed. Not only do these activities reinforce concepts young children are already learning, such as counting, matching, and telling time, they also offer children the opportunity to ask questions, talk about their feelings, and feel connected to their deployed parent.

This activity book is broken into four sections, with activities appropriate for each stage of deployment:

Getting Ready for Deployment 3

Deployment 33

Getting Ready for Reunion 67

Reunion 89

Find a place where you and your child can focus on the activities. Take time to ask your child what he or she is feeling and answer questions in an age-appropriate way. Come back to this book as you enter each stage of deployment, from packing and saying goodbye to welcoming Dad home. This process will help children feel as if they are a part of the process and will help them prepare for what's coming next.

For more about supporting children during deployments, go to www.survivingdeployment.com. *My Mom's Deployment: A deployment and reunion activity book for young children* is also available from Elva Resa Publishing. Visit www.elvaresa.com.

My Dad's Deployment: A deployment and reunion activity book for young children
Text and Illustrations ©2009 Elva Resa Publishing. All rights reserved. No part of this publication may be reproduced without prior written permission of the publisher.

Written by Julie LaBelle for Elva Resa Publishing, except prayer (p. 8) and story (p. 57) written by Alexander Pavlicin.
Illustrated by Christina Rodriguez and Elva Resa staff for Elva Resa Publishing.
Design by Andermax Studios.
Special thanks to our testers: Erin, Alli, Elsa, Sean, Ryan, Ben, and Alexander.

ISBN 978-1-934617-07-6
Printed in United States of America.
 2 3 4 5 6 7 8 9 10

Bulk discounts available.
Elva Resa Publishing
8362 Tamarack Vlg Ste 119-106, St Paul, MN 55125
http://www.elvaresa.com
http://www.MilitaryFamilyBooks.com

Getting Ready for Deployment

What Does "Deploy" Mean?

Deployment means your dad will travel away from home to serve his country and do his job. He might be gone a long time. When he is done with this job, he will come home to you and your family.

Other People Who Have Deployed

Do you know other people who have deployed?
Write down their names and draw their faces.

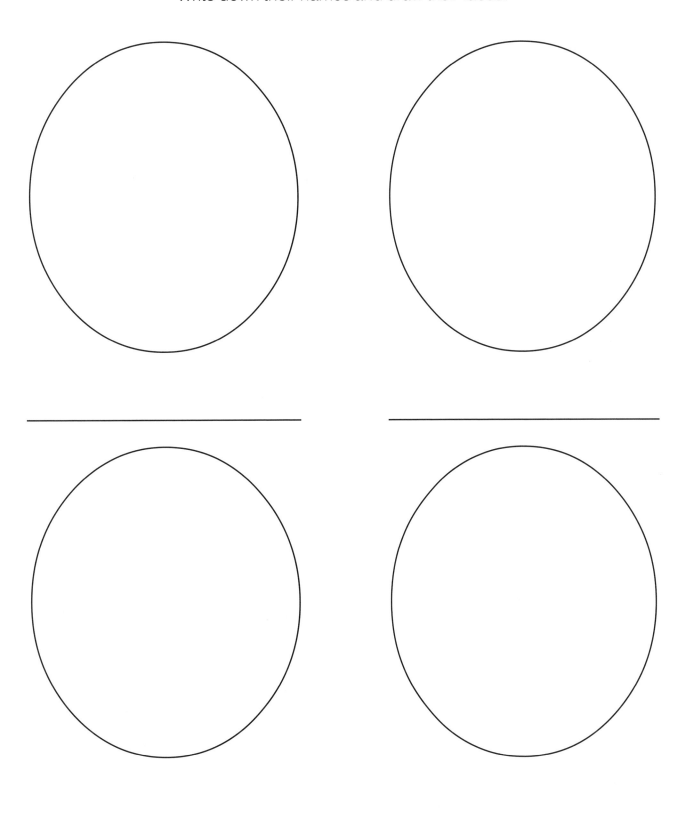

Map of the World

Color the map. Draw a heart where you are.

Draw a heart where your dad will be. Connect the hearts.

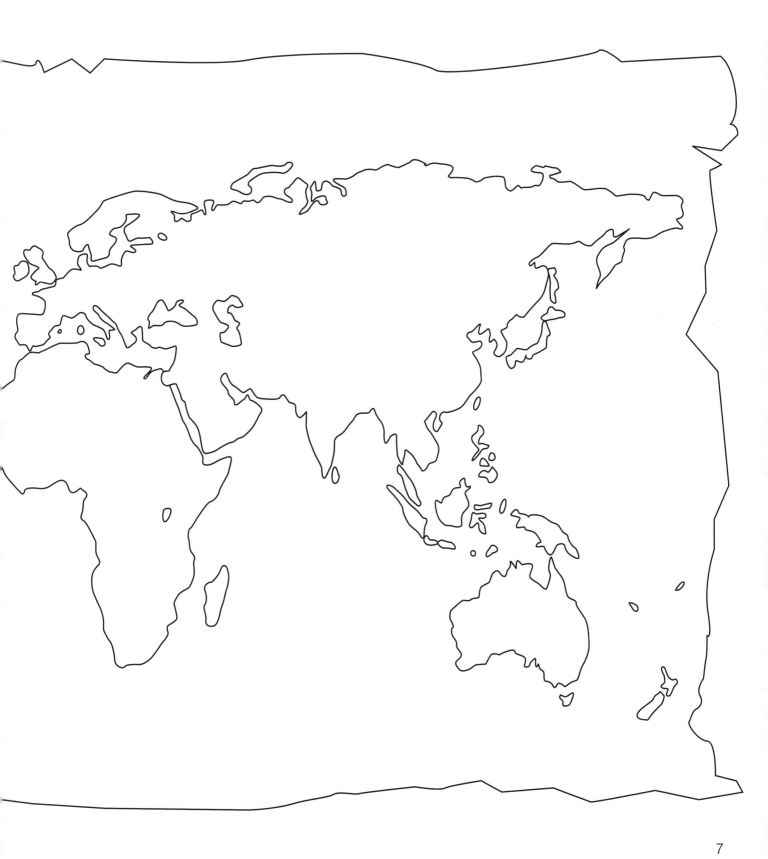

Prayer for Safety

Sometimes it feels like there is nothing you can do to help when someone you love is going away for a while. One thing you can do is say a prayer. You can say this prayer or make up your own prayer.

Dear God,
Please help Daddy stay safe while he is deployed. Help him to come home soon. Watch over our family while Daddy is gone. Please keep Daddy close to us through our prayers and the ways we stay in touch.
                                        Amen.

We Can Stay in Touch

Staying in touch means that even though you cannot see each other in person, you can still do things together and speak to each other. You can still tell each other about your day and say I love you in different ways.

Trace the words.

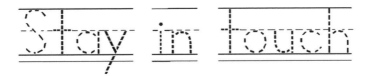

Circle the ways you can stay in touch with your dad.

Talk on the phone

Send special packages

Write and mail letters

Share photos

Color and mail pictures

Email each other

Things Dad and I Can Do Before He Deploys

Dad has lots of packing to do to get ready for his deployment. You have things you can do with Dad to help you feel ready, too. Color the pictures to show things you and Dad can do together before he deploys.

☺ We can call each other so I can practice talking on the phone.

☺ We can give each other something special. During the deployment we can look at our gifts and think of each other.

☺ We can take a walk together and talk about deployment.

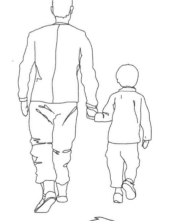

☺ We can talk about ways we can stay in touch.

☺ I can sit on Dad's lap and tell him how I feel.

☺ We can make a project together that will help me remember Dad after he leaves.

More ideas (write them here and draw a picture below) _____

_____

_____

Our Favorite Place

Together draw a picture of a favorite place you like to go together. Color your picture.

Our Favorite Things to Do

Together draw a picture of a favorite thing you like to do together. Color your picture.

We Will Both Sleep Under the Same Moon

We Will Both Wake Up to the Same Sun

Make A Patriotic Mailbox

While Dad is deployed, you will probably send each other cards and letters. This patriotic mailbox will give you a special place to keep letters to and from Dad.

What you will need:

★ Empty shoebox

★ Red, white, and blue colored paper

★ Star stickers

★ Glue stick

★ Scissors

★ Tape

To make your own mailbox:

1. Cover the shoebox with white paper. Cover the lid and bottom separately.
2. Cut a 4-inch square of blue paper and add star stickers. Attach the square with the stars to the upper left corner of the box lid.
3. Cut 1 inch strips of red paper. Glue to the top of the box to make the flag stripes.
4. Write MAILBOX on the side of your box. Use your mailbox to store letters to and from Dad.

Messages In A Jar

It's nice to get a message from Dad, even on days when he can't write or call. Together, cut out the messages below and put them in a jar. While Dad's deployed, pull out a message at bedtime or whenever you want to hear from him. You and Dad can create your own messages on the extra strips and by cutting up blank paper to write on.

I think of you each day.

Goodnight. I love you!

Did you brush your teeth?

You are my sunshine.

Messages

Deployment Time Capsule

A time capsule is a special place where you can keep important things you want people to see in the future. You can make your own deployment time capsule -- all it takes is a box or jar and some things you want your dad to see when he gets home!

You will need:

A shoebox or jar with a lid

Photos

A note to your dad

A list of your favorite things, such as your favorite:

- ☺ Food
- ☺ Movie
- ☺ Book
- ☺ Song
- ☺ Activities
- ☺ Friends
- ☺ TV show
- ☺ Stuffed animal
- ☺ Clothes
- ☺ Toy

Wrapping paper

Tape

To make your capsule:

Inside your box or jar, place your photos, note, and list of favorites. Close the lid and wrap with colored paper. Mark the date on your box and write "Deployment Time Capsule." When your dad comes home, you can open your time capsule together. You can talk about how things have changed and how they have stayed the same.

Color the American Flag

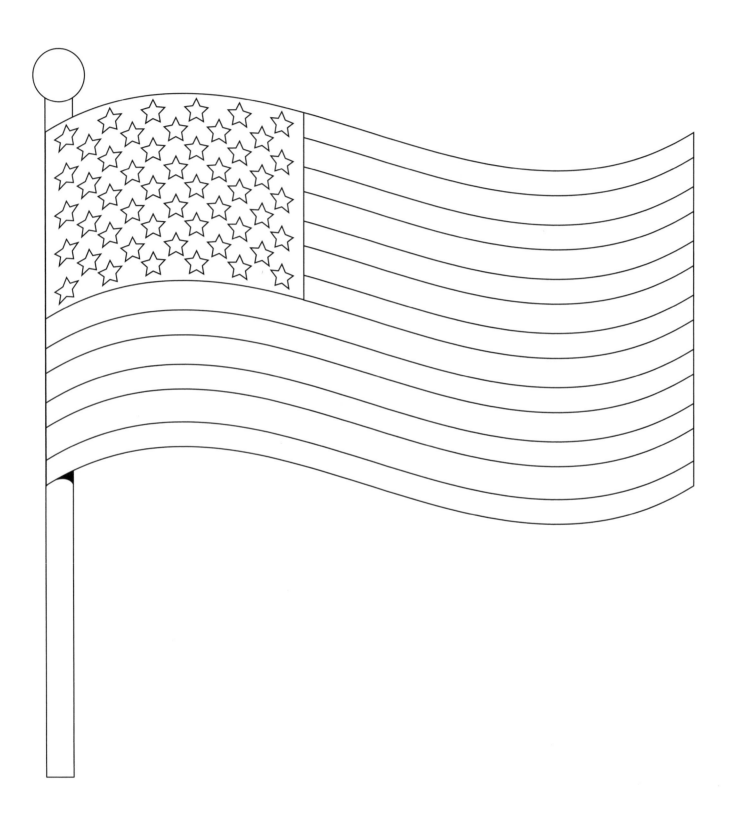

A Few Good Surprises
(Dad - Don't Look!)

When Dad's clothes are packed, ask Mom to help you tuck in a few surprises. Some ideas:

- ☺ A picture you colored folded into his shirt
- ☺ A laminated picture of you
- ☺ A piece of candy tucked in his pocket
- ☺ Other special things: _____

Ssshhhhhh! Keep it a surprise!

Learn Dad's Alphabet

People in the military use words for different letters of the alphabet. When it is noisy, it is easier to hear words like Alpha, Bravo, and Charlie than A, B, and C. What other words can you think of to go with each letter? Write the word or draw a picture.

A   Alpha

B   Bravo

C   Charlie

D   Delta

E   Echo

F   Foxtrot

G   Golf

H   Hotel

I   India

J   Juliette

K   Kilo

L   Lima

M Mike

N November

O Oscar

P Papa

Q Quebec

R Romeo

S Sierra

T Tango

U Uniform

V Victor

W Whiskey

X X-ray

Y Yankee

Z Zulu

Connect The Dots

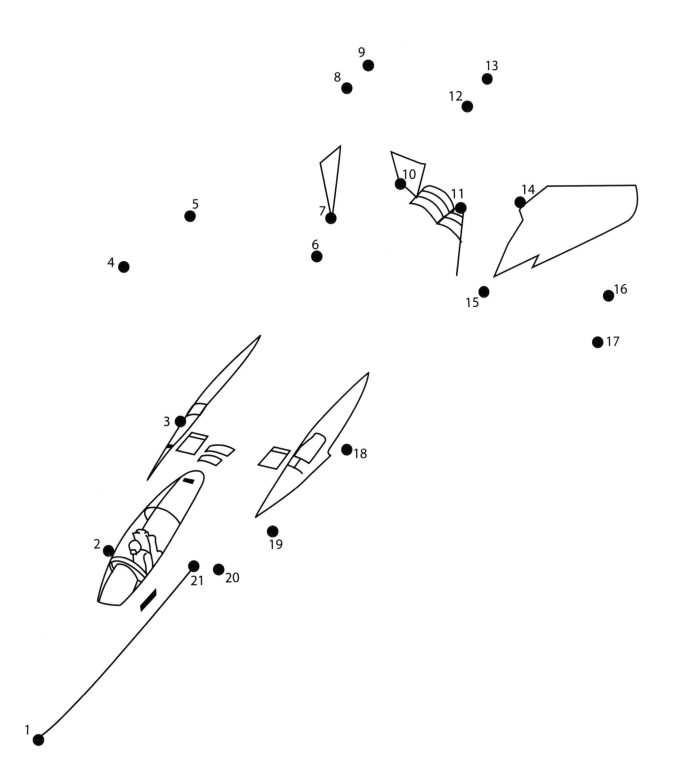

Connect The Dots

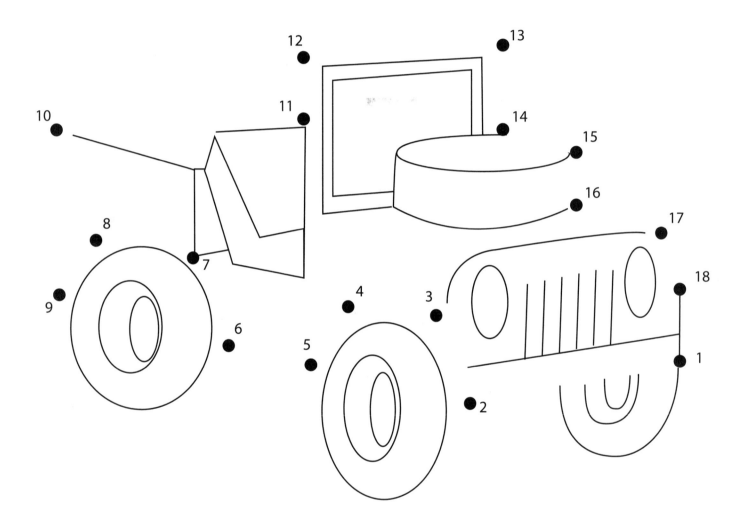

Connect The Dots

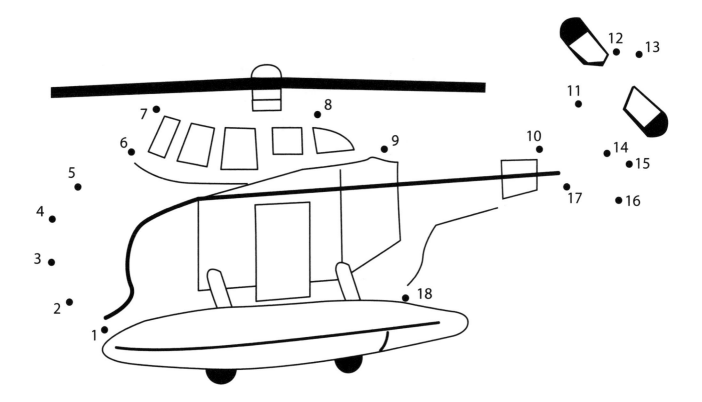

Connect The Dots

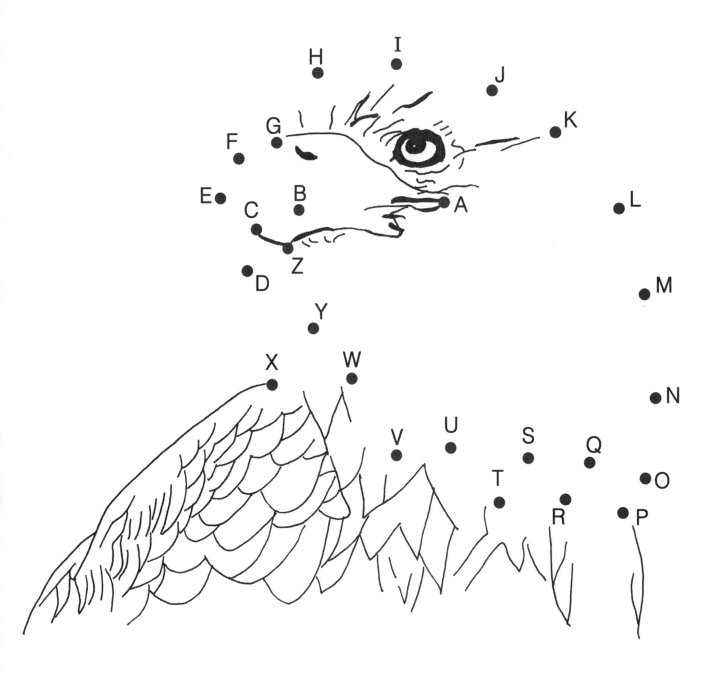

Packing Bags

Help Dad find things he needs to put in his bag for his trip. Find and circle each of the words from the list below. Words may appear forward or backward, horizontally, vertically, or diagonally.

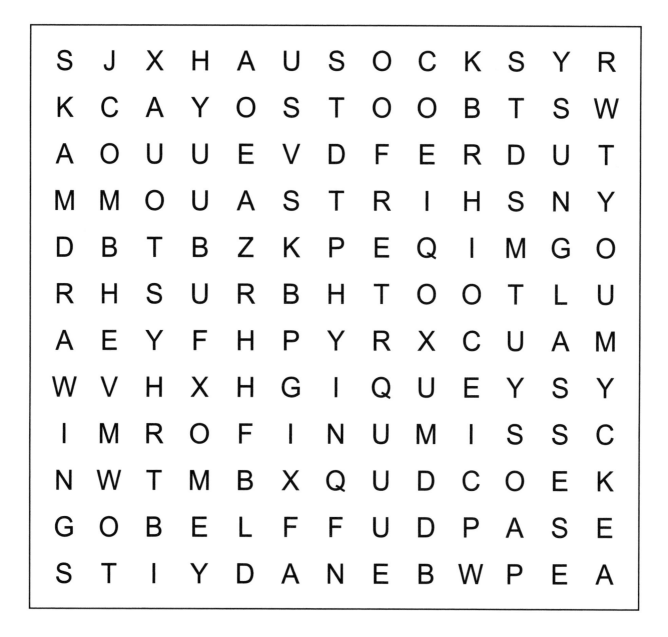

```
S  J  X  H  A  U  S  O  C  K  S  Y  R
K  C  A  Y  O  S  T  O  O  B  T  S  W
A  O  U  U  E  V  D  F  E  R  D  U  T
M  M  O  U  A  S  T  R  I  H  S  N  Y
D  B  T  B  Z  K  P  E  Q  I  M  G  O
R  H  S  U  R  B  H  T  O  O  T  L  U
A  E  Y  F  H  P  Y  R  X  C  U  A  M
W  V  H  X  H  G  I  Q  U  E  Y  S  Y
I  M  R  O  F  I  N  U  M  I  S  S  C
N  W  T  M  B  X  Q  U  D  C  O  E  K
G  O  B  E  L  F  F  U  D  P  A  S  E
S  T  I  Y  D  A  N  E  B  W  P  E  A
```

book   comb   duffle   shirts   socks   toothbush
boots   drawings   photos   soap   sunglasses   uniform

29

On the Day Dad Leaves

Circle the things you might do together when Dad leaves.

Hug

Eat a special meal together

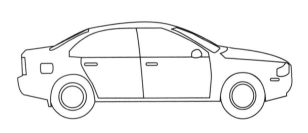

Drive in a car

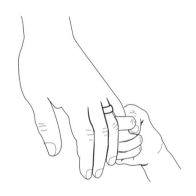

Hold hands

Say goodbye at home

Say goodbye someplace else

After We Say Goodbye

Circle the things you might do after saying goodbye to Dad.

Take a walk with Mom

Eat ice cream

Play with friends

Snuggle and watch a movie

Give and receive lots of hugs

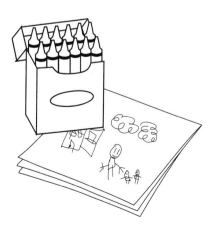

Draw pictures

What Comes Next?

Draw what comes next in the pattern.

□ ○ □ ○	
A A B B C C D	
(tent) (helicopter) (tent) (humvee)	
△ ▽ ♡ △ ▽	
(family) (boot) (sun) (family) (boot)	
♡ ☆ ☆ ♡ ☆	

Deployment

Feelings

Circle the face that shows how you feel about Dad's deployment today.

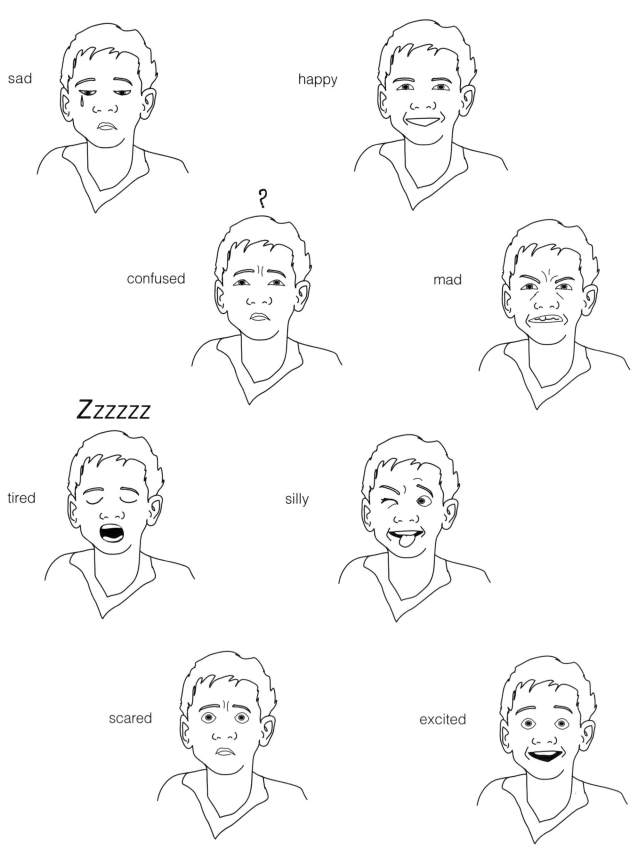

sad

happy

confused

mad

Zzzzzz

tired

silly

scared

excited

When I Feel Scared

Circle the things you might do when you feel scared.

Tell someone how I feel

Ask for a hug

Keep a flashlight by my bed

Cuddle with someone I love

Say my prayers

Watch a happy movie

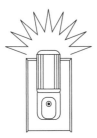

Turn on a night light in my room

Read a special book

When I Feel Angry

Circle the things you might do when you feel angry.

Kick a ball outside

Run really fast, back and forth in the yard

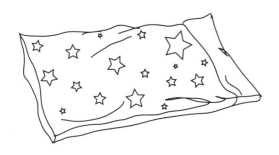

Squish a pillow

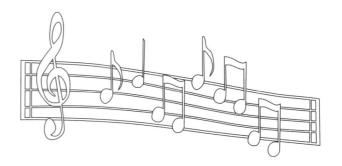

Sing a favorite song

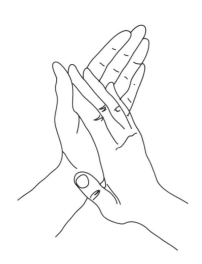

Clap my hands

Dance around to music

When I Feel Sad

Circle the things you might do when you feel sad.

Cuddle with a special blanket
or stuffed animal

Draw a picture of how I feel

Ask for a hug

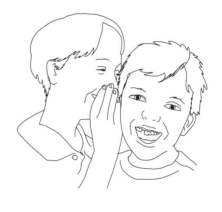

Think of a funny joke or story

Ask questions if I don't understand
or I am worried

Play with a good friend
who can cheer me up

Helping Around the House

Make a list of the ways you can help around the house while Dad is away.

☑ Set the table

☐ Help fold clothes

☐ Make my bed

☐ Pick up toys

☐ _____

☐ _____

When Dad Calls

Think about what you would like to say to Dad if he calls on the phone.

You can practice on a toy phone.

Wishing Trees

Even on the days when you can't talk to Dad on the phone or send emails, you can still wish good things for him. On a wishing tree, you write a wish or prayer and attach it to the tree. There are many ways to make a wishing tree. Here is one way:

What you will need:

★ Large piece of construction paper or poster board
★ Colored paper
★ Crayons or markers
★ Glue stick
★ Scissors

To make your wishing tree:

1. Draw a tree on the large piece of paper or poster board.
2. Using the colored paper, cut out shapes of hearts, stars, leaves, or ribbons.
3. Write a wish or prayer for Dad on each shape you cut out.
4. Glue the wishes onto your tree.
5. Hang your wishing tree in your room, on the refrigerator, or another special place where you can see your wishes and add more whenever you want to.

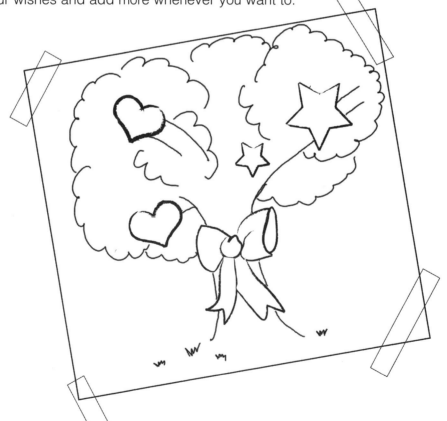

For more wishing tree ideas, go online to www.elvaresa.com/wishingtree.html

Make a Wish!

Color the wishing tree, then write a special wish on the ribbon at the bottom.

Based on the book *The Wishing Tree* by Mary Redman and Christina Rodriguez. www.elvaresa.com/wishingtree.html

Some Things Stay the Same; Some Are Different

When Dad is away, some things change, but other things stay the same. Write the words or draw a picture to describe what you do when Dad is home and what you do when he is deployed.

When Dad is home:

We eat _____

We go to bed at _____

We play _____

We _____ on Saturday mornings

When Dad is deployed:

We eat _____

We go to bed at _____

We play _____

We _____ on Saturday mornings

What stays the same? What is different?

Some Things Stay the Same; Some Are Different

Color all the things you can do when Dad is home.

Circle the things you still can do when Dad is deployed.

Eat pizza

Read books

Go to the park

Wrestle with Dad

Watch a movie

Do a puzzle

Play a game

Snuggle

What stays the same? What is different?

Scavenger Hunt

Hunt for these items to send in your next care package to Dad. Check off the box when you find the item.

❏ A picture of me

❏ A story I made up

❏ A leaf or flower from the yard

❏ A picture I drew

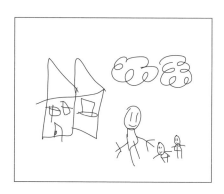

❏ A sticker

❏ A special treat

Messages From Home

Tear out this page and ask your friends and family to write special messages on the back to send to Dad. Have them sign their names. You may need to use more sheets of paper for all your messages. Decorate your pages and send them to Dad.

Messages From Home

Messages From Dad and His Friends

Tear out this page and mail it to Dad. Ask him to collect autographs and messages from his buddies and send them back to you.

Messages From Dad and His Friends

Photo Collage of Dad and His Buddies

When someone is away for a long time, it is nice to have lots of pictures around to remind us of what the person looks like and what we love about the person. While Dad is deployed, you can create a special poster of Dad and some of the people he works with.

What you will need:

★ Pictures of Dad and his buddies
★ Poster board
★ Glue stick
★ Markers and stickers

To make your poster:

1. Ask Dad to send you pictures of himself and his buddies.

2. Decorate the border of the poster board using stickers and markers.

3. Use glue stick to attach pictures of Dad and his buddies to the poster board.

4. Hang your collage on the wall for your family and friends to see.

A Picture of Me

Draw and color a picture of yourself. Remember to add hair, eyes, and the clothes you like to wear. You can send your picture to Dad or show it to him when he comes home.

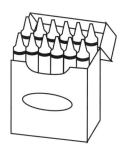

_____
(Sign your name)

My Hand

Trace your hand below. Color or paint your hand drawing. Decorate it with rings, fingernails, bracelets, or a watch. You can send your hand picture to Dad or show it to him when he comes home.

Time Difference

Around the world, we have different time zones. For example, when it is 9:00 a.m. in California, it is 12:00 p.m. in New York, and it is 5 p.m. in England. You and your dad both eat and sleep, but do you do it at the same time? With an adult, figure out the difference in time between where you live and where Dad is deployed.

At home the time is: Where Dad is, the time is:

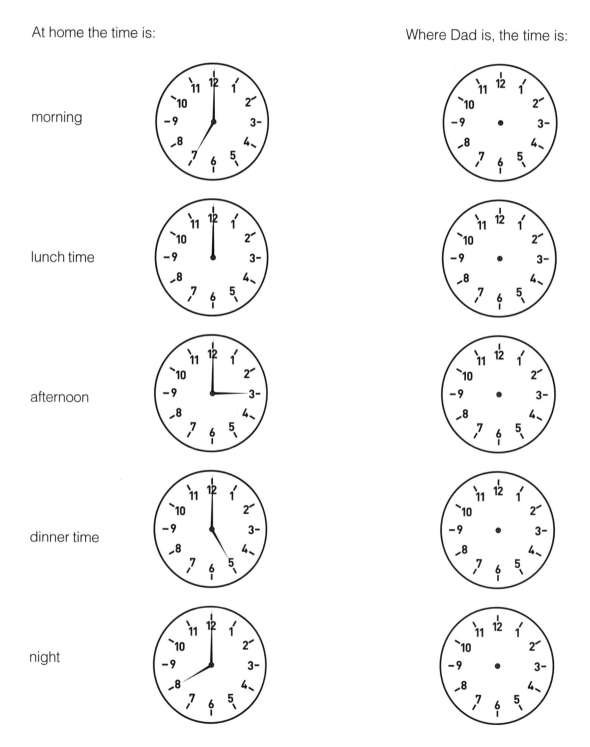

morning

lunch time

afternoon

dinner time

night

Time Difference

Draw a line to show what Dad is doing while you are waking up, eating lunch, playing with friends, eating dinner, and sleeping.

When I am: Dad is:

Learning About Where Dad Is Deployed

Find out more about where your dad is deployed. Ask an adult to help you find out the answers to these questions:

My dad is deployed to _____(base/city)_____ , which is in

_____(country)_____ . The people there speak _____(language)_____ ,

and this is how they say "hello": _____ . Many people there really like

to _____(an activity)_____ . The weather there is _____(hot/cold)_____ ,

so Dad needs lots of _____(item of clothing)_____ .

This is the most interesting thing I learned about where Dad is deployed:

_____

_____

_____

_____

_____

What Does It Look Like There?

What does it look like where Dad is deployed? Ask Dad to send you pictures or with an adult go to the library or to a web site to see pictures of the military base, city, or country where Dad is deployed. What is the same or different from where you live?

Draw a picture of what you think it looks like where Dad is:

★   ★   ★   ★   ★   ★   ★   ★   ★   ★   ★   ★   ★   ★   ★

★   ★   ★   ★   ★   ★   ★   ★   ★   ★   ★   ★   ★   ★   ★

What Does Dad Do at Work?

Color the pictures to show what Dad might do today at work.

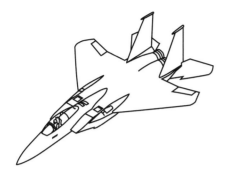

Fly an airplane

Eat lunch

Ride in a helicopter

Sleep in a tent

March in formation

Read a letter

Drive a truck

Think about me!

Goofy Story

Fill in a word for each question.

1. A food I like to eat: _____

2. An interesting color: _____

3. How I feel today: _____

4. My favorite animal: _____

5. Something I do in the morning: _____

6. A strange noise: _____

7. A friend's name: _____

8. What I say when it's time for a bath: _____

Now match the word for each numbered question above to the numbered lines below to create a goofy story.

One day, I was _____(5)_____ with my _____(4)_____ when I heard

a loud _____(6)_____. I looked up and saw a giant bucket of

_____(2)_____ _____(1)_____. My _____(4)_____

starting eating the _____(2)_____ _____(1)_____ so my friend

_____(7)_____ shouted "_____(8)_____." And that is why I am

feeling _____(3)_____ today.

Things I Am Learning To Do

Everyone learns new things during a deployment. With an adult, keep track of some of the things you are learning during your dad's deployment.

☐ I can count to _____
(date)

1 2 3 4 5

☐ I can spell my name _____
(date)

☐ I can tie my shoes _____
(date)

☐ I know my address _____

_____
(date)

☐ I know my phone number _____
(date)

☐ I know my ABCs _____
(date)

A B C

☐ I can zip a zipper _____
(date)

☐ I can button a button _____
(date)

Other things I am learning to do:

Learning to Spell and Write

Mom   Mom   Mom   Mom

Dad   Dad   Dad   Dad

I Love You   I Love You

Aa Bb Cc Dd Ee Ff Gg

Hh Ii Jj Kk Ll Mm Nn Oo

Pp Qq Rr Ss Tt Uu Vv

Ww Xx Yy Zz

(my name)

My Favorite Things

Sometimes our favorite things change over time. What are your favorites today?

Food:

Books:

Activities:

Friends:

Songs:

Movie or TV show:

Look At Me Grow!

With a grownup, make a growth chart to keep track of how much you grow while Dad is away.

You will need:

★ 5 sheets of cardstock or paper
★ Tape
★ Marker
★ Ruler
★ Stickers

How to make your growth chart:

1. Tape the pieces of paper together, end to end, until it is taller than you are.

2. Hang the chart on the wall.

3. Ask Mom or another adult to mark the paper in inches and feet, measuring from the floor up the wall.

4. Every month ask someone to mark your height. Stand up straight with your feet flat on the floor and your heels to the wall. Look straight ahead.

5. Be sure to write the date next to your height marker.

You can show Dad how much you've grown when he comes home!

Or, you can ask Mom to take a picture of you in the same spot every month. Look at the pictures with Dad when he gets home so he can see how much you've grown.

Hugs Hugs Hugs

Hugs are wonderful! Who can you hug today?

My Little Book of Dad

Color the pictures and cut them apart. Then staple the pictures together in any order and use them to tell a story about your dad.

Book of Dad

My Little Book of Symbols

Color the pictures, then cut them apart and staple together in the order you want for your book. Talk with a friend about what each of the symbols means to you.

Getting Ready for Reunion

Things I Want To Do When Dad Comes Home

Circle the things you would like to do with Dad when he comes home.

Hug

Read a book

Eat ice cream

Cuddle

Get tucked in bed

Sing a happy song

Go for a walk

Eat our favorite meal together

Dad and Me Finger Puppets

You'll need a washable marker and two fingers. With an adult's help, draw Dad's face on one finger and your face on the other finger. Now you and your little finger puppets can talk to each other. Pretend you are talking to Dad when he comes home. What would your puppets say to each other?

Ways to Welcome Dad Home

Color the pictures to show ways you would like to welcome Dad home.

Fly the American flag.

Make a giant poster with
    "Welcome Home Daddy!" on it.

Tie yellow ribbons around the house and yard.

Make some of Dad's favorite foods.

Get out Dad's favorite game to play.

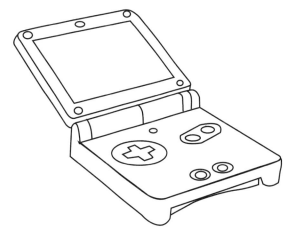

Pick up my room and toys. Help Mom get the house ready.

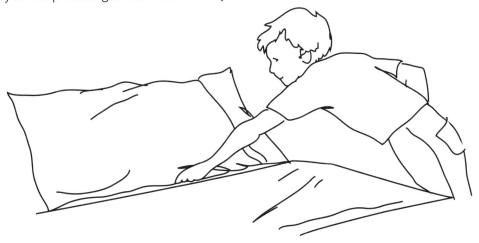

Welcome Home Card

Make Dad a welcome home card.

You will need:

★ Paper

★ Stickers

★ Crayons or markers

★ Your creativity!

To make your card:

1. Fold your piece of paper in half.

2. On the front of the card, draw and color a picture or write "Welcome Home."

3. On the inside, write a note or draw a picture for Dad. Sign your name.

4. Put your card in a special place to give to Dad when he comes home.

Welcome Home Poster

Make Dad a welcome home poster.

You will need:

★ Poster board

★ Markers or crayons

★ Stickers

★ Balloons (optional)

To make your poster:

1. Ask an adult to help you write a big welcome home message on your poster.

2. Color your poster and add pictures and stickers.

3. Blow up the balloons and tape to the corners of your poster.

4. Hang the poster where Dad will see it and give him a great big welcome!

Sidewalk Chalk Welcome Home Sign

Make a sidewalk chalk sign to welcome Dad home.

What you will need:

★ Colored chalk

★ A sidewalk or driveway

★ An adult to help

★ A camera (optional)

To make your sidewalk chalk sign:

1. With an adult, find a safe place on the sidewalk or driveway where you can use your chalk to draw.

2. Draw pictures and write "Welcome Home" using your chalk.

3. When Dad comes home, show him your masterpiece!

4. If it might rain before Dad will see your sidewalk chalk sign, take a picture to show him later.

Paper Loop Chain Decoration

Decorate for homecoming with a red, white, and blue paper loop chain.

You will need:

★ 9 sheets of construction paper (3 red, 3 white, and 3 blue)
★ Ruler
★ Tape or stapler
★ Scissors

To make your paper loop chain:

1. Cut your paper into strips.
2. Loop a red strip into a circle and ask an adult to help you tape or staple the ends together.
3. Loop a white strip through the first red loop and tape or staple the ends.
4. Loop a blue strip through the white loop and tape or staple the ends.
5. Continue your red, white, and blue pattern until you've used up all the strips.
6. Decorate your front door or another special place with your chain.

Match & Rhyme

Match the words that rhyme.

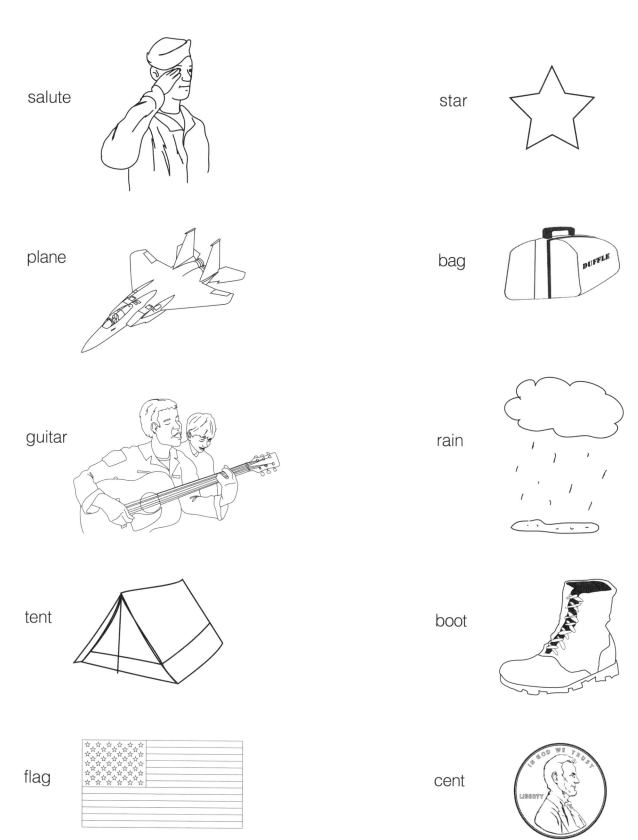

salute

plane

guitar

tent

flag

star

bag

rain

boot

cent

How Many?

Draw a line from the number on the left to the number of objects that match it.

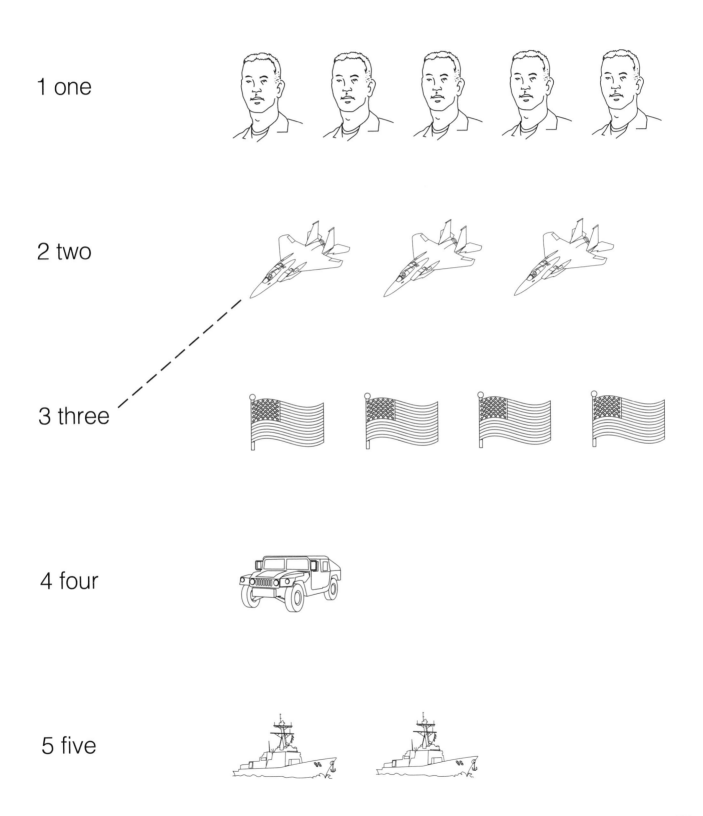

1 one

2 two

3 three

4 four

5 five

What Does Not Belong?

Circle the item in each row that does not belong with the others.

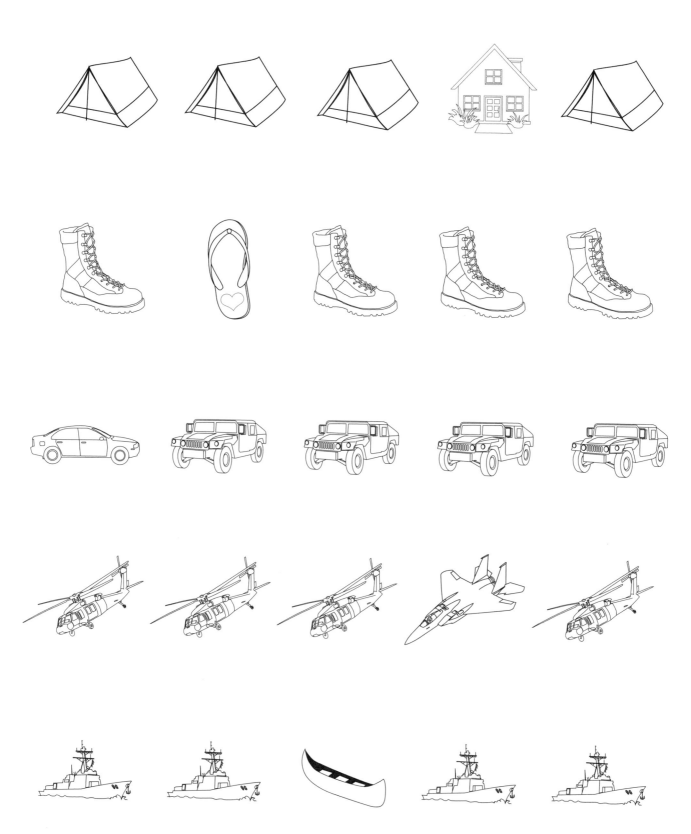

Matching

Draw a line from the item on the left to the object on the right it goes with.

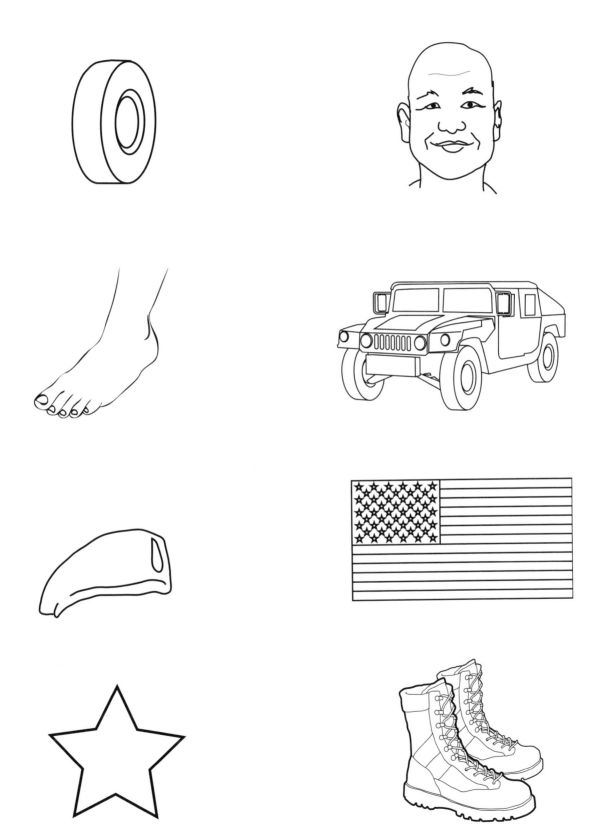

I'm Proud of My Dad

There are lots of reasons to be proud of your dad. Think of some of the reasons you are proud of him. Then draw a picture of your dad and tell why you are most proud.

- My dad is strong
- My dad is kind
- My dad protects America
- My dad is my hero
- My dad teaches me things

- My dad is brave
- My dad is smart
- My dad protects me and my family
- My dad takes care of us
- My dad is my best buddy

I am most proud of my dad because:

This is a picture of my dad:

What Kind of Hugs?

On homecoming day, what kind of hugs would you like best? Circle all the kinds of hugs you would like to give or receive.

How I Feel

Circle the faces that show how you might feel on homecoming day.

How Will Dad Get Home?

Circle the ways Dad will travel to get home.

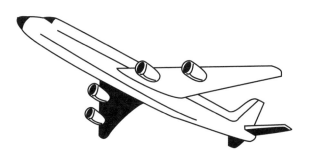

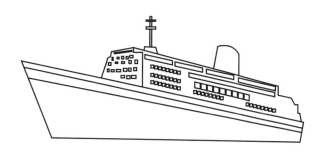

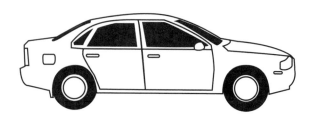

What Should I Wear?

Pick out the clothes you want to wear on homecoming day. Color the clothes you think would make a nice outfit to wear when you welcome Dad home.

Ways I Have Changed

You've grown while Dad was gone. What else about you has changed since Dad deployed? Draw two pictures, one that shows you before Dad deployed and one that shows you now.

Before Dad deployed	Now

How Might Dad Be Different?

Just as you have changed while Dad's been gone, some things about Dad might have changed, too. Talk with an adult about the ways you think Dad might be different.

He might:

- ★ have a tan
- ★ like new foods
- ★ have new buddies

- ★ want to be quiet sometimes
- ★ feel a little grumpy and tired
- ★ know new things

Draw a picture of how you think Dad might be different when he comes home.

Which is the Biggest?

Circle which one is bigger in each row.

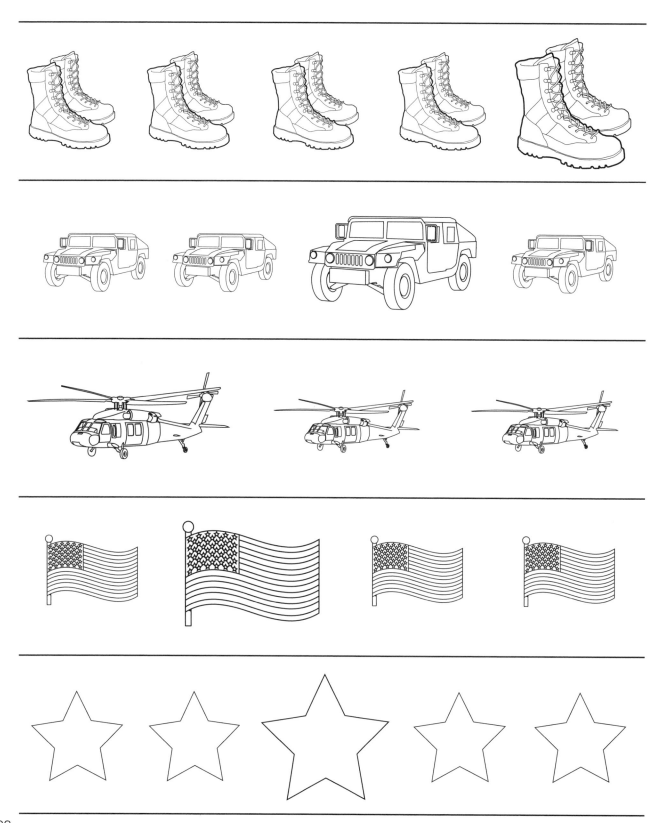

Reunion

Help Dad Find His Way Home

Draw a line from Dad to you to help him find his way home.

Help Mom and Dad Find Each Other

Draw a line from Mom to Dad
so they can give each other a big hug and kiss!

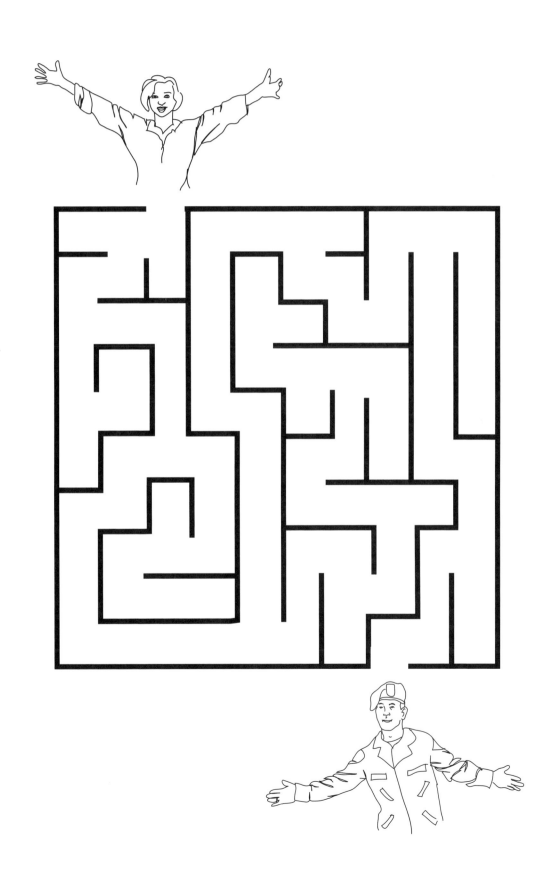

Things We'll Do On Homecoming Day

Circle the things you will do the day Dad comes home.

Wash my face

Brush my teeth

Comb my hair

Make my bed

Put on my special clothes

Get ready for big hugs!

A Picture of Dad and Me on the Day He Comes Home

Draw a picture or use glue stick to put a photo of you and Dad in the frame.

Ways I Can Help Dad Feel Welcome at Home

Color the pictures and circle the ways you can help Dad feel welcome.

Get his favorite pajamas and slippers ready

Tell him how much I love him

Ask him to play games

Let Dad rest and get used to being home

Let Mom and Dad spend
some quiet time together

American Flag

Color the American flag by matching the numbers to the correct colors.

1=Red
2=White
3=Blue

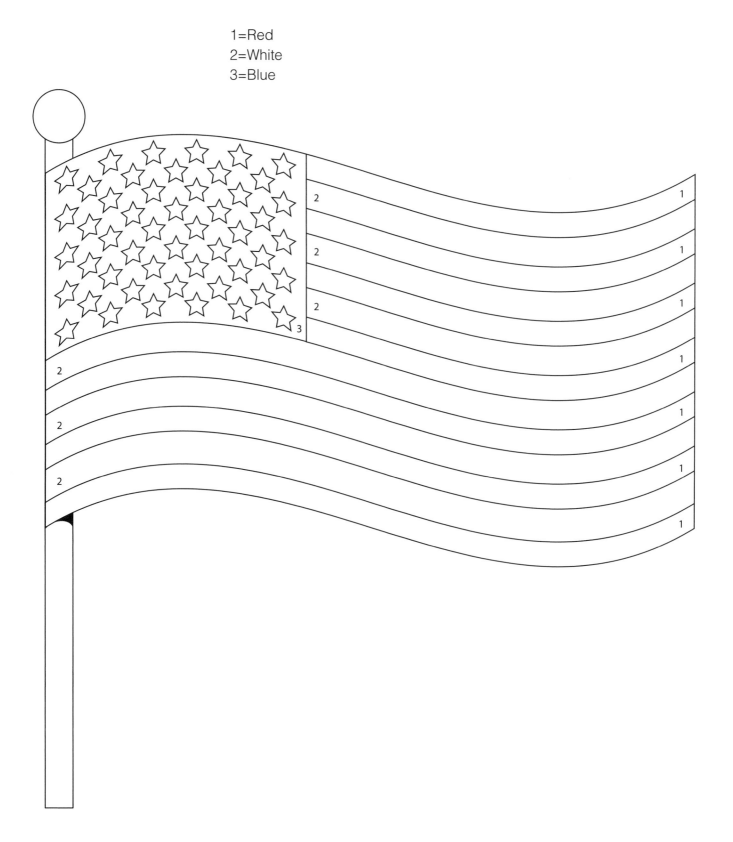

Match the Hugs

Color the pictures and circle the two that match.

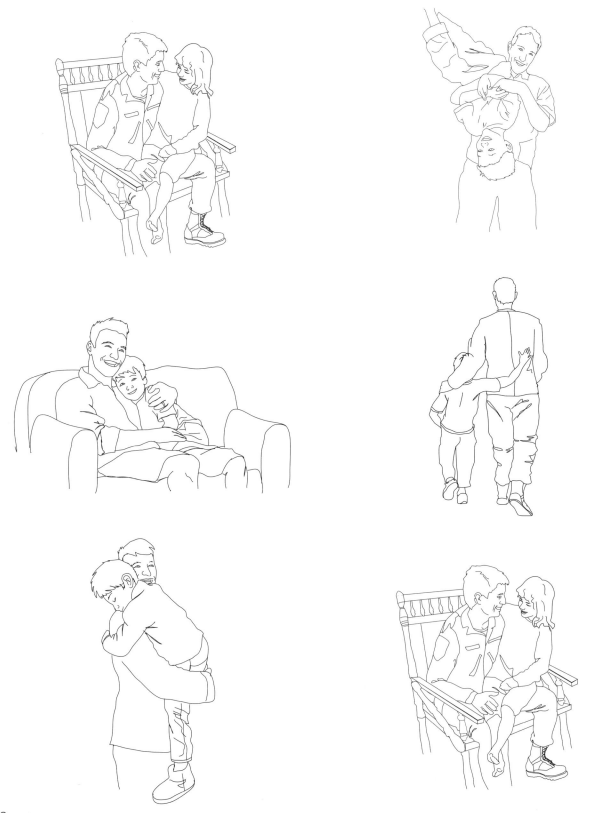

More Things to Do With Dad

Circle the things you want to do with Dad now that he's home. Color the pictures.

Sing a favorite song

Eat a favorite food

Read a favorite book

Watch a favorite movie

Play a favorite game

Go to a favorite park

Sharing With Dad

When Dad comes home everyone will need to share.

Circle the things you will share.

How Many?

Color the correct number in each row.

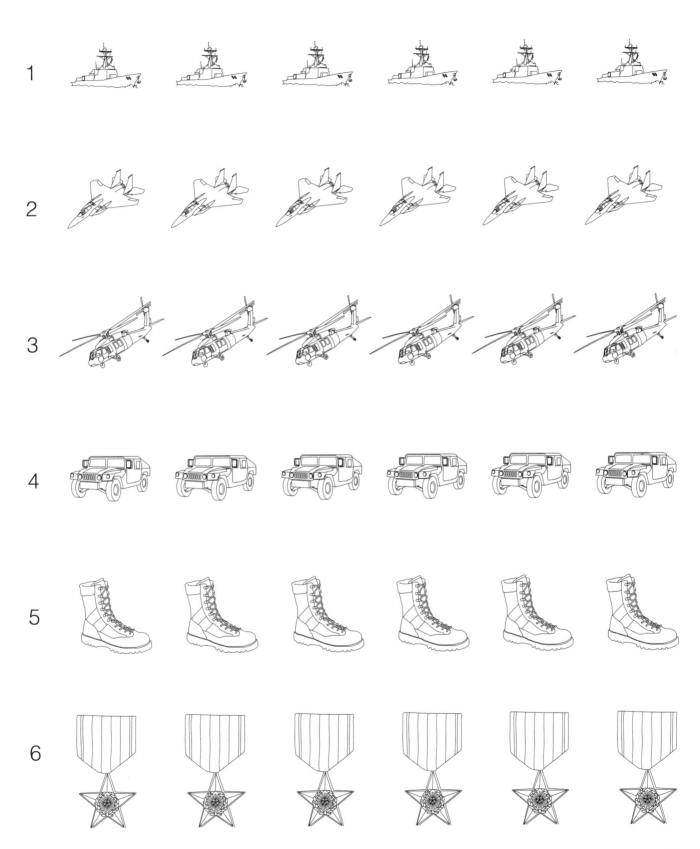

1

2

3

4

5

6

Color-By-Number

Color the picture by matching the numbers to the colors listed below.

1=green
2=yellow
3=blue
4=red

WELCOME
HOME

God Bless America

Color the picture.

Matching

Color the two planes that are the same.

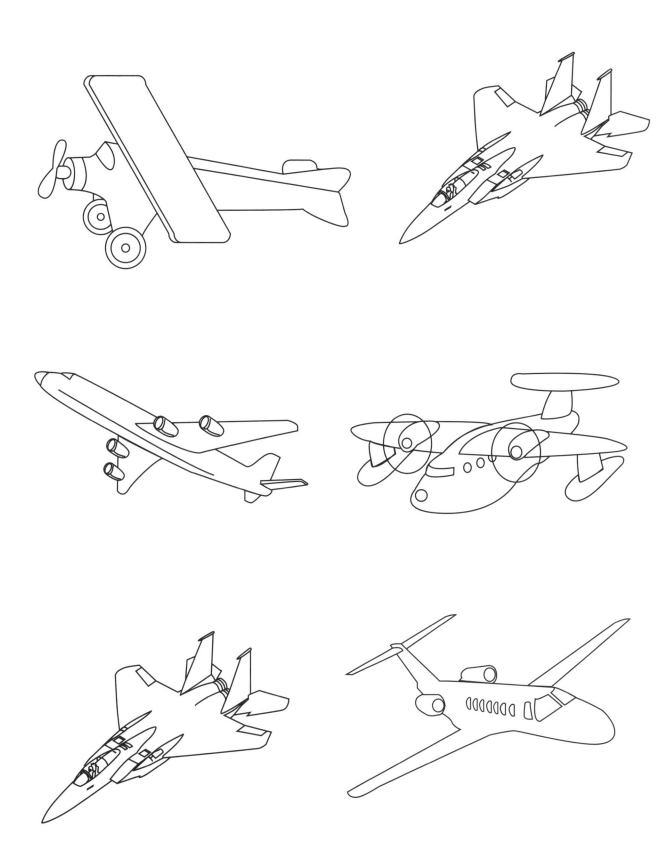

Matching

Color the two ships that match.

Dad's Story

Ask Dad to tell you a story about his deployment.
Draw a picture about Dad's story.

What I Can Do Now

Share with Dad the new skills you learned while he was gone.

Hidden Picture

Find the hidden flag. Color the picture.

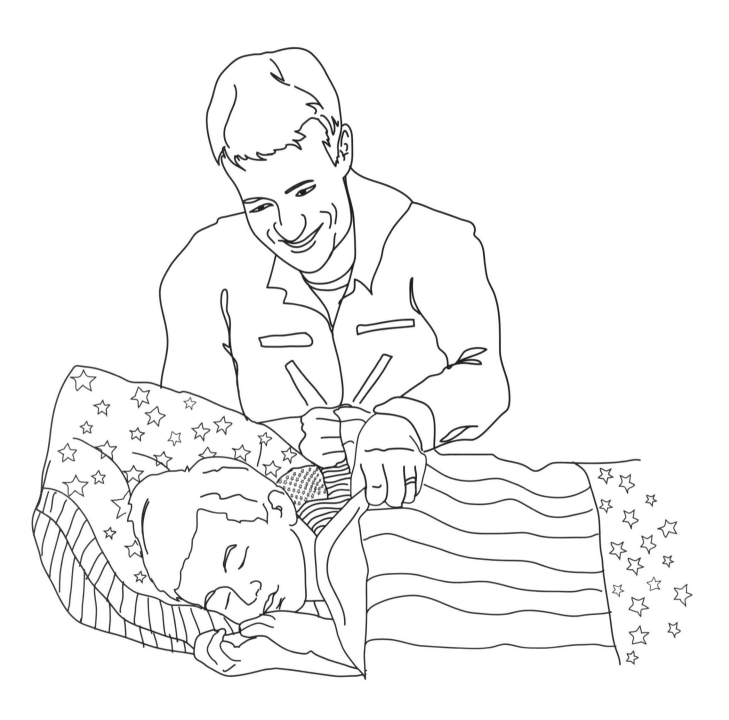

Open the Deployment Capsule

It's time to open your deployment time capsule with Dad! Gather your family around and open your time capsule. Look at the things you put in your box or jar.

Are you different now than when you started your time capsule? How have things changed? What stayed the same?

Things Our Family Learned Together

There are many things your family might have learned during Dad's deployment.

★ To be brave and help each other.

★ To rely on each other and ask each other for help.

★ To be patient and kind.

★ To stay in touch.

★ To give great hugs!

Draw a picture to show some of the things your family learned during Dad's deployment.

We Are Thankful

Draw pictures of some of the things you and your family are thankful for now that the deployment is over.

You Did It!

Draw a picture of your favorite part of this deployment.

Draw a picture of your least favorite part of this deployment.

CERTIFICATE OF ACHIEVEMENT

Awarded to:

_____

For learning so much during Dad's deployment to _____

and for being an all-around great kid!

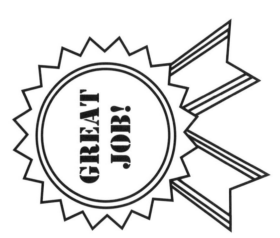

GREAT JOB!

Awarded by:

_____

Awarded on:

_____